Poetry In Motion

ARVEENA SONI

New Delhi • London

BLUEROSE PUBLISHERS
India | U.K.

Copyright © Arveena Soni 2024

All rights reserved by author. No part of this publication may be reproduced, stored in a retrieval system or transmitted in any form or by any means, electronic, mechanical, photocopying, recording or otherwise, without the prior permission of the author. Although every precaution has been taken to verify the accuracy of the information contained herein, the publisher assume no responsibility for any errors or omissions. No liability is assumed for damages that may result from the use of information contained within.

BlueRose Publishers takes no responsibility for any damages, losses, or liabilities that may arise from the use or misuse of the information, products, or services provided in this publication.

For permissions requests or inquiries regarding this publication, please contact:

BLUEROSE PUBLISHERS
www.BlueRoseONE.com
info@bluerosepublishers.com
+91 8882 898 898
+4407342408967

ISBN: 978-93-5741-754-9

Cover design: Muskan Sachdeva
Typesetting: Rohit

First Edition: January 2024

Dedication

To my parents...my role models who taught me to believe in myself and to never give up on my dreams.

To my family, my loved ones, my friends and my well-wishers who always believed in me and inspired me to keep on following my passions.

To all my dedicated readers, great writers and poets who always appreciated my work and encouraged me to keep on writing.

And finally, to love and life itself..... my greatest teacher as well as my biggest inspiration. Every single lesson learnt from love and life is nothing but poetry for me...to be mesmerized forever.

"But those love poems were written in her eyes for him right from the very beginning......

It's just that he didn't stare, dare or care enough to read ....

until her vulnerable loving heart couldn't hold them anymore and finally began to bleed... 🖤✍️*ArVi...!!"*

Contents

1 She Is Poetry In Motion... 1

2 When Someone You Love Leaves You... 3

3 Uniquely Beautiful. 5

4 Beautification.... 7

5 Places. 9

6 Ocean Of Emotions…... 11

7 Burning Pyre.... 13

8 Wind Chime…. 15

9 Love Song…. 17

10 Loving Him Feels Like.... 19

11 Mad Passionate Love.. 21

12 His Arrival and His Departure..... 23

13 How Finding And Losing Love Feels Like... 25

14 Being Drunk On Thou Intoxicating Love......................... 27

15 His Love Did To My Vulnerable Heart...... 29

16 She Sounds Like........ 31

17 Memories…. 33

18 Someone's Poetry..... 35

19 How Can I Ever Give Up On Thou Love...... 37

20 Light As Well As Darkness.. 39

21 Big Love... 41

22 Priority…... 43

23 Why..45
24 Rewrite Every Sad Love Story..........................47
25 Poetry Is Meant To Be Felt..................................49
26 Eternal Stay...51
27 Be My Wish That Comes True............................53
28 Journey..55
29 Be My Devoted Reader.......................................57
30 A Handwritten Letter To A Stranger.................59
31 Girl Like Her Is Found Only In Poetry..............61
32 Insane Love...63
33 Eternity..65
34 He Is To Me What Rain Is To Dark Clouds.......67
35 Dream Or Nightmare..69
36 Passionate Book Lover..71
37 Shallow River He Was...73
38 One Fine Day..75
39 I Love Him Just Like..77
40 Telepathy...79
41 Library...81
42 Everything That Looks Like Some Art..............83
43 Her Love Was Just Like Her Poems…Her Art...85
44 Unconditional Love..87
45 Her Eyes Recite Love Poems..............................89
46 Merging Two Diverged Rivers Into An Ocean..91
47 Her Love And Her Light.....................................93

48 Irony Of Love...95
49 Where Does All That Love Go.......................................97
50 Love Lasts Even When Life Doesn't............................99
51 Leave Me Like..101
52 Love So Deep...103
53 Love Of A Poetess..105
54 Mosaic...107
55 Intrigued By Those Twinkling Stars............................109
56 Mind Vs Heart..111
57 Monday Morning…..113
58 Written In Braille...115
59 Forgetting Thee Feels Like..117
60 Friendship Vs Love..119
61 She Finally Let Him Go...121
62 His Undeniable Presence Or His Unbearable Absence......123
63 Her Silent Love Speaks To His Heart.........................125
64 He Left Me With So Much Of Poetry
   (Diminishing Poem) 127
65 Being a Priority..129
66 Ends Up To Your Pages...131
67 Never Really Missing From Me..................................133
68 The Glue..135
69 Turn Them Into Your Poetry......................................137
70 Everything Tragically And Terrifically Beautiful
   About Her...139

71 Love Is Never About	141
72 She Keeps On Filling	143
73 In Each Other's Thoughts And Prayers	145
74 How Stubborn Your Love Is	147
75 Stuck On Love	149
76 But I Love Him	151
77 Loving You Even More	153
78 Find Someone Who Feels Like Some Love Song	155
79 Waves Of An Ocean	157
80 In Every Love Story	159
81 Hidden Treasures	161
82 Promise	163
83 Immortal Love	165
84 Love Poem She Is	167
85 Thou Eyes	169
86 Solace	171
87 Her Love Is Divine	173
88 Book Lover	175
89 Wild And Dense Forest	177
90 Love Is A Raging Fire	179
91 Love Her Loud	181
92 She Is Made Up Of	183
93 Being An Extremist And An Empath	185
94 I Will Let You Set The Pace	187
95 Loving You In My Dreams	191

96 Where Can We Find True Love? 193

97 Museum. 195

98 Crescent Full Moon.... 197

99 Love...199

100 Bookmark…. 203

1
She Is Poetry In Motion...

"*Flowing non stop like rivers.....*
Flying high like free birds without any feathers or wings ....
Quite awakened about all spiritual and deep meaningful things....
Touching and soothing the souls just like music does........
Healing thousands of hearts that are falling apart, though her own heart is always on storms....
As if ,at it's very depth, it holds some hurricane of emotions.....
Still so calm and silent at the surface just like deep oceans..........
For some, a mystery.....while for others, an untold story.........
If not everyone else , atleast poets can surely relate ....
A passionate girl like her to poetry...ArVi..!!"

Arveena.

2
When Someone You Love Leaves You...

"So what do you do when someone you love leaves you...as if, you are nothing more than an empty hallway......

You decorate every single empty corner or leftover passage or blank wall of your vulnerable heart with bittersweet memories of their love and then turn this so called hallway into a beautiful museum.........

Yeah , that's what you really do...............

For just because someone didn't appreciate your love and your innocent heart and left you to dance all alone in rain.............

Doesn't mean you will let all the deep and pure love you have for them just go in vain.........

You show this world how a warrior and stubborn heart like yours refuses to be torn or fall apart.........

So you turn everything that hurt you or tried to break you into your power..............

By setting yourself as an example of a phoenix or a warrior........

By becoming yourself only, a mosaic or a masterpiece of an art....ArVi..!!"

Arveena.

3
Uniquely Beautiful...

"Indeed.....

She had a unique beauty and light......

But the kind of light, only people that have been through darkness can see.......

And the kind of beauty , only the person who is a bit broken can feel.......

And that was the real thing she realized over the years.............

That almost everyone had been through some darkness .....

And was a bit broken too....ArVi..!!"

Arveena.

4
Beautification....

"But no one has ever defined me, the way she did..........
And no one has ever refined me, the way she did..
My life was so full of meaningless words.....
She embraced me with the music of her undying love.........
Turned all those empty words into mesmerising lyrics........
And turned me into her poetry ....
And if you ask her......
For her, i am not just her lover.......
But the love poem that she will mesmerize forever...ArVi..!!"

Arveena.

5
Places...

"*But I love him in places where he doesn't exist physically..........*
But occupies all the space emotionally.........
Like in music, in memories, in prayers ,in dreams, in heartaches and in my poetry .....
For in all these places, i can't deny his inevitable presence even in his absolute and unavoidable absence.........
Like i just said...............
I love him in places where he doesn't exist physically.......
But occupies all the space emotionally ....ArVi..!!"

Arveena.

6
Ocean Of Emotions....

"Oh darling ,look at your heart........
Oh...so pure, serene and eternal ...
As if, some masterpiece or some unique piece of an art.........
The ultimate depth that it holds and the hidden treasures that it befolds....
Oh, so obvious for them to dive and swim in those small ponds and rivers....
For you being an ocean of emotions deserve only perfect sailors...ArVi…!!"

Arveena.

7
Burning Pyre....

"Inhaled him and just forgot to exhale out....
And now , every now and then.....
Those longings for his love .....
Those love fantasies and burning desires....
Ignite a raging fire inside my vulnerable heart like a burning pyre.....
The more i try to blow it off, the more it is ignited everytime ...
Turning every bit of mine into ashes......
Everytime unforgettable memory of his love flashes.......
Since then, day and night i am craving for his single touch....
Oh never knew i could love and miss someone so much......
But somehow he slipped away for he couldn't handle such an intense love and madness.....
And so, he left me hanging with just two options. .....
Either to keep on choking myself with the leftover smokes of his burning love...
Or to spend the rest of my life just breathless...ArVi..!!"

Arveena.

8
Wind Chime....

"My heart is just like a wind chime......
Making no noise or voice...just standstill ....
Where his memories are the soft breeze.....
That slowly and gradually...moves or turns it on...........
And so, the melody of love........
Plays on and on and on......ArVi..!!

Arveena.

9
Love Song....

"Hey beloved.....
So now you only tell me.....
What should i do.......
How do i forget about You ......
And how can i ever get over you.........
When in every single love song i sing or listen to........
If the lyrics is me, the music is you.......
If the music is me, the lyrics is you........ ArVi...!!"

Arveena.

10
Loving Him Feels Like....

"Loving him feels like......
Having your favourite cup of coffee on a cold rainy winter morning.....
And missing him feels like..
It's bittersweet aftertaste......
And no matter.....
How bitter it turns out to be.....with time......
You don't give up on it somehow....
For deep inside you know it quite well......
You are already addicted to it by now....ArVi...!!"

Arveena.

II
Mad Passionate Love......

"Oh this mad passionate intense love.....
So cruel and unfair..........
For even when he is no more here.......
I feel him almost everywhere..........
Even in the air i breathe........
The rain that falls all over me......
The wind that touches me..........
The poems i read or write...........
And the songs i listen to or hear........
Oh , such an incredible presence even in someone's absence.............
Is so rare....
So rare, that it's hard to bear........ArVi..!! "

Arveena.

12

His Arrival and His Departure.....

"Indeed....His arrival added meaning to my life....
For he rose in my dark grey dull and vast sky .....
Just like the sun rises at the outbreak of the dawn......
But i can't deny.....
That even his departure from my life......
Was equally mesmerizing and breathtaking ....
For it was just like the sun sets down in the evening....
Being tired of shining and burning......
A sort of dying rage, a fading spark........
Gradually turning everything around me so silent, serene and dark......
Somewhat painful, yet so meaningful and beautiful....
So beautiful that i can never forget it's sight.......
Even if it means nothing, but dying of all my shimmering lights.......
And beginning of all those dark nights ......
Truly said ...
Sunsets are as beautiful and meaningful as a sunrise....ArVi..!!"

Arveena.

13
How Finding And Losing Love Feels Like...

"How finding love feels like.......?

Finding love feels like...as if , after a decade of dark nights , there is an outbreak of dawn....

And beginning of a fresh enlightened morning just too full of hope and light....oh so beautiful , lively and bright.............

That it feels worth every mess, chaos, struggle or fight.........

How losing love feels like.......?

And losing love feels like ....

As if, the only sun in your vast sky sets down silently.........

Turning all it's crimson red hues into deep blues......

Slowly and gradually, losing all it's real charm and spark...........

And suddenly, in the blink of an eye....

There's nothing left ,but your sky is all pitch dark......ArVi..!!"

Arveena.

14
Being Drunk On Thou Intoxicating Love.........

"Being drunk on thou intoxicating love is to be there with thee in all your insane dreams or madness , is to erase and take away all your hurting memories or sadness.......

Is to dance to the rhythm of thou love in all those heavy storms and rains ....

Is to embrace with my whole heart all your darkness and pains ...

Is to taste all the mess and the chaos thee offer or gift me along with thou beautiful and vulnerable heart ....

And found it all damn bitter, still keep on drinking it anyway...........

For by now............

I am already addicted to this slowly killing poison of love that comes with just no antidote........

Yeah, by now i am already addicted to all the mayhem just beyond your wildest imagination or thought.........ArVi..!!"

Arveena.

15
His Love Did To My Vulnerable Heart......

"His love did to my vulnerable heart what a raging sea does to it's sea shore...............

Tidal waves of his memories keeps on coming and going back as and when they wish.......

With all it's intensity and density, always crashing me, washing me, sweeping me off my feet...

Turning all my dried up and half dead emotions wet and alive again....

Reminding me off and on of all the heartaches, memories , hurt and pain....

Leaving thousands of scars, bruises and traces on the very surface of this deserted heart 's sea shore ....

Making me wish and long everytime for him

to come back just once more....ArVi..!!"

Arveena.

16
She Sounds Like.........

"And she sounds like .....

A hope to hopeless....

A home to homeless.....

And heartbeats to heartless. ....

Oh, she is just born to express and not to impress......

Read her, learn from her.....

Get inspired from her and love her........

But don't you ever try to possess. ......

Beauty like her is hard to find.......

Yes she holds that power to paint thousands of beautiful images in your mind.....

For those who just don't understand her, she is merely an arrangement of words. ....

But for those who love her, she is the most beautiful melody......

And all the poets and the poetess around call her poetry...........ArVi..!!"

Arveena.

17
Memories...

"Your memories come and go like those vigorous waves of the sea.....

touching my heart and soul, sweeping me off my feet....

Dragging me down deeper and deeper...

With it's unexpected strong flow without any force of gravity, push or pull your side.. ....

And i am trying so hard every time to save my fall.......

And it makes me wonder for how long i would be able to stand and survive this terrible beautiful disaster.........

For nobody ever taught me how to swim in the ocean of love......

Especially, when the storms are on.....ArVi...!! "

Arveena.

18
Someone's Poetry.....

"And he said to me......
But had i met you before...
Had i been some beautiful character in your life story.....
Then trust me, would not have let you become someone's poet.......
For a girl like you just deserves to be someone's poetry.....ArVi..!!"

Arveena.

19
How Can I Ever Give Up On Thou Love......

"How can i ever give up on thou love.....
How will i ever give up this fight.........
When even when i tried to give up on you......
My eyes just refused to give up on your sight........
As if , i am a moth drawn towards you for my self destruction.......
Where you being the only worthy flickering light.... ArVi..!!"

Arveena.

20
Light As Well As Darkness.....

"*On some days....*

I am as fragile and vulnerable as petals of a rose or wings of a butterfly.....

While on other days ....

I am as strong as thorns of a rose or wings of a phoenix.........

But somehow on both days and in both ways..........

I appreciate and embrace my uniqueness......

For i know it damn well.............

That i am made up of...

Both my light as well as my darkness....ArVi...!!"

Arveena.

21
Big Love..........

"Oh that big love, what a beautiful disaster....
So magical, real, unconditional , pure and divine........
That even when your beloved ignores you, hurts you or pushes you away....
Even when you feel the pains to the extreme and your heart bleeds endlessly in love, it still whispers in it's every single heartbeat.......
Oh darling , I am perfectly alright and fine for the pleasure is all mine... ArVi..!!"

Arveena.

22
Priority.....

"Too many options surrounding his life…
Knowing the hard fact ….
Her mind and her heart just refused to become his choice….
For whether you call it as recognition of self worth..
Or just her insanity………..
But that crazy girl always believed …..
That she was born to be………
Nothing less than someone's priority…..ArVi..!!"

Arveena.

23
Why.......

" Why it's you only and not those who love me and care for me that set my soul free?

Why you only can make me laugh, why you only can make me cry?

Why can't i forget you the way you do?

Why can't i let you go no matter how hard i try?

You love me too..!!

Why i always feel like trusting this and why i keep on feeding myself with this self told lie?

And now it really scares me to think if i ever be able to kill your memories until the day i die...ArVi…!!"

Arveena.

24
Rewrite Every Sad Love Story............

"And she sighed and whispered......
If only, I can rewrite every sad love storybook in reverse order................
Then ending of every such love story would be happily ever after..............
Indeed...
There will be only innocence, fun, love and laughter........
And if nothing else.....
At least there will be no pains, distrust, betrayal or heartaches..........
As lovers then would be nothing but strangers......ArVi…!!"

Arveena.

25
Poetry Is Meant To Be Felt..............

"She was a mystery........
Who didn't want to be solved.......
A wild spirit who didn't want to be caged or tamed........
A kind of insanity that no more seeks for any clarity.......
And a crazy mess of all deep jumbled words ....
That don't want to fit in any box just to make a complete sense...........
Because more than some mystery..........
She was undeniably an anthology, a poetry...............
And poetry is never meant to be understood..........
Just meant to be felt ......
To it's real depth meant... ArVi…!!"

Arveena.

26
Eternal Stay........

"But she always wanted to hold him close and a little longer than anyone had ever held him before ....

I mean so close and so long that he just can't walk away or get away even if he wishes to or tries to............

And so.....

She held him in her thoughts, in her music, in her prayers and in her poetry.....

And that's how she made him stay....

Oh what an eternal stay, no chances of him getting away...ArVi…!!"

Arveena.

27

Be My Wish That Comes True.......

"You touched my life in explicit ways like some electrifying magnetic spark....

As if , you knew it damn well that his damn soul was lost somewhere in some shell or dark.......

You filled my life with peace , happiness and light.....

As if, you knew it damn well that this girl was struggling somewhere with some real chaos or fight.......

Indeed i owe you a lot for all this undeniable care, friendship and unconditional love....

As for me it's nothing less than some blessing from the heaven above...

But right now i just can't figure out so far who you really are......

As in my vast grey sky, you feel like some twinkling shooting star.......

So you only tell me, can i really trust you.....??

Yeah, you only tell me......

Will you ever be my innocent wish that will really come true......ArVi..!!"

Arveena.

28

Journey.........

"But loving him always felt like a journey to me........
A journey that never ends for it's a journey with no dead ends.......
A journey where i am driven by my passion..........
Oh so natural, travelling there without a pause has become my obsession......
A journey where i don't need any other companion........
Can travel all alone on my own.....
So who cares, if midway, i found some road bumps, rocks or stones ....
A journey so full of ups and downs, highs and lows, mountains and valleys......
Oh so tiring and long that walking continuously in between lights and shadows finally made me so confident and strong.........
A journey where i usually lose my mind, my sanity, my ability to think straight, my very track.....
For it's a journey once started and now there is just no traverse or going back........
A journey that made me forget about every other damn destination.......
A journey that is as much my dangerous venture as much it is my only salvation......
Yeah loving him always felt like a journey to me........
A journey that never ends for it's a journey with no dead ends...ArVi…!!"

Arveena.

29
Be My Devoted Reader......

"And she said.........
So i am an open book........
Behind closed doors.......
Written in braille just for you.........
Read me as deeply as you can.......
And as longer as you can............
Before the dawn breaks ....
And we both wake up finally from our dream of love.........ArVi...!!"

Arveena.

30
A Handwritten Letter To A Stranger........

"A handwritten letter to a stranger......
Don't you ever fall in love with her.........
She is just priceless like love, so you just can't earn her..........
Her soul is already set on fire, so your spark just can't burn her..........
You can only mesmerize her for the poetry she is, but you can't impress her ....
A spirit so wild, untamed and free that you just can't possess her...........
Her heart is just too much stormy, an ever raging ocean.........
Diving in would only mean drowning in her deep emotions.........
She already had her enough share of intoxicating love and pain............
So she will never fall in love with anyone ......
She will never trust another soul so blindly once again............
Alas, all your genuine intentions and all hard efforts will be just in vain............
She has raised her love game just too high by now .....
So you will only lose.....
Trust me, there is no real gain..........
A handwritten letter to a stranger....
Yeah don't you ever fall in love with her......ArVi..!!"

Arveena.

31
Girl Like Her Is Found Only In Poetry......

"They asked me...

So where shall we find a girl like her?

I smiled and replied.....

You will find her.....

In rainbows after rains.....

In healings after pains........

In sunshine right at the outbreak of the dawn.....

In the courage when someone walks the journey of this life all alone......

In flowers eternal colors and fragrance....

In someone's strength, patience, forgiveness and endurance.........

In innocent smile of a child.......

In the soar of birds flying free and wild.......

In a lover's true and deep emotions....

In the hidden treasures and mysteries of an ocean......

In peace that you feel and experience right after doing meditation.....

In adrenaline rush, when someone recklessly follows his or her ultimate passion........

No , you just won't find a poem like her anywhere in history ....

But you will surely find her in a poet's love quills, proses and poetry.....ArVi...!!"

Arveena.

32
Insane Love.....

"What an insane love it is........

He has never seen her tears..........

He has never felt her pains..........

Infact, he was the only one who ever left her to dance all alone in darkness and heavy rains.......

And now when she is shining so bright and appeared before everyone as rainbow in the vast sky after all those storms and fights.....

She still gives all the credit to him only ....

As if, he was her only divine sunlight......ArVi...!!"

                                                              Arveena.

33
Eternity.......

"One moment of love shared long time back.....
One flower of love grown long time back.......
One star of love shone long time back......
One song of love sung long time back.........
And then, thousands of poems and stories written over that single beautiful memory. ....
To mesmerize and feel it again and again. ...
Whenever you are happy or in extreme pain......
Just to make it sure that love never fades away......
Even when the lovers themselves walk away......
Indeed, it is truly said.....
Some stories are meant to be written or engraved ....
To make them eternal forever....ArVi...!!"

Arveena.

34
He Is To Me What Rain Is To Dark Clouds......

"*He is to me what rain is to a dark cloud.......*
Hardly together still always inseparable........
And every time i am just too full of him......
Every time this rain overflows through this dark cloud.....
Like some thundering and lightning , i just scream out loud...
And then, i let him go and i let it rain.....
To let go of all the hurt, love , anguish and pain.....
Until i hold him firmly once again............
As i already said........
He is to me what rain is to a dark cloud.......
Hardly together still always inseparable.....ArVi…!!"

Arveena.

35
Dream Or Nightmare......

"And she said.......
For after all this time, i was still not sure................
If you were a dream or a nightmare.....
Still a mesmerizing dream worth chasing any more ....
Or have turned into a terrible nightmare meant to be forgotten to the core.....
A precious gem to be treasured more and more...
Or a poisonous empty shell meant to be left just untouched at the shore.........
A lighthouse that will shelter this lost sailor of love like a warm and cozy home.............
Or a tsunami crashing wave that will drag me and just leave me to get drown all alone in this life 's raging storm...........
For after all this time , i was still not sure...........
If you were a dream or a nightmare...ArVi...!!"

Arveena.

36
Passionate Book Lover.....

"Oh that mesmerizing look ....
Of that anthology , that unique book.......
Indeed , i admit and i confess ......
That i was spellbound at first sight only by the intoxicating beauty of her outer cover ......
But it's only when i actually peeked into her mind , her eyes...
And read the contents of her heart and soul......
That in true sense, i became that book 's real passionate lover....ArVi..!!"

Arveena.

37
Shallow River He Was........

"It's only...
When i saw and felt his cold and dried up emotions.....
That i realized.......
Might be he was merely a shallow river.........
While a mermaid like me was born to dive....
Only in deep and eternal raging oceans....ArVi...!!"

Arveena.

38
One Fine Day............

"And then one fine day........
Unknowingly and unexpectedly......
Someone will come along ....
May be a friend, a well-wisher or a complete stranger.......
Who will hold your hand ......
Will listen to you like no one else ever did without judging a bit ....
Will mend and stick together all damaged and broken pieces of your loving heart ......
And that person will help you to forget about the one who tore you apart.........
And then......
Day by day, you will start forgetting about all the hurt and the pain......
And then slowly and steadily........
Will learn to trust, smile and love all over again.........ArVi..!! "

Arveena.

39
I Love Him Just Like.......

"I love him.........
Just like the clouds love the rain.......
Just like a masochistic love the pain.....
Just like the oceans love the storm.....
And i am as much confident about the power of my own love......
As much i am secured to always let him go.............
For I know, no matter what happens .....
No one can ever stay away for too long.....
From his or her very sweet home.......ArVi...!!"

Arveena.

40
Telepathy........

"For sometimes, the most deepest form of love.......
Is just the silent knowing between two hearts and souls.....
That both of them care............
And if need arises, both of them will always be there.........
No matter how much there is distance between them........
And whatever might be their different so called final destinations............
They will always be feeling each other ....
For somehow , somewhere , one way or other......
They will always be looking in the same directions ....
While sharing same love, emotions, understanding and deep affection ...ArVi...!!"

Arveena.

41
Library...........

"They all got fascinated by the charm of her face........

Were hypnotized by the glow in her melancholic eyes and were intrigued by all her eternal grace...........

And found her worth reading as a book or worth mesmerizing her as a poetry...........

But it's only when they really peeked into her mind, heart and soul ....

That they found ....

That she was rather an anthology, a vast library........ArVi...!!"

                                                                Arveena.

42
Everything That Looks Like Some Art..........

"But i see you in all the places where one can see only with his or her heart.....

Like in music, in poetry and in everything that looks like some art..........

In shadows of the moon, in waves of the ocean........

In my every single deep emotion that feels like some devotion........

In my chase, in my pause.....

in every why, what if , if only and because.........

In my insanity, in my madness.......

Sometimes you are there in my joy as well as in my sadness............

In my dusk, in my dawn........

In the moments i let you go and in the moments i choose to hold on......

In my darkness , in my light.....

In my peace and serenity and in every heart's struggle or fight.......

Yes i see you in all places where one can see only with his or her heart.....

Like in music, in poetry and in everything that looks like some art........ArVi..!!"

Arveena.

43

Her Love Was Just Like Her Poems...Her Art........

"Her love was just like her poems, like her art ......
Just too raw, too deep and always flowing recklessly through her heart....
For somehow , just like her poems ......
She never understood how to edit it, where to end it....
How to manipulate it and how to decorate it.....
Oh , always so real and intense, i mean so raw, real and intense.........
That she didn't really know how to let it make a complete sense ......
How to make it more attractive or appealing..........
How to make it more expressive or revealing.........
For somehow, both her poems and her love.........
Had their very origin from her heart 's true emotions ......
And from their unexpressed and unexplainable feelings....
Yeah, her love was just like her poems like her art........
Just too raw, too deep and always flowing recklessly through her heart..ArVi…!!"

Arveena.

44
Unconditional Love.....

"Unconditional love is.......
When two souls are interconnected ......
And are drawn to each other...........
In an unimaginable and unexplainable way ....
Unseen, unheard.....never shown, never said.....
Nothing to lose and nothing to prove......
But one heart is always aware of the silent love and care by the other loving heart ....
At every single point of time, right from the very start......ArVi...!!"

Arveena.

45
Her Eyes Recite Love Poems.......

"Every single deep mesmerizing love poem........
Hidden and written in my melancholic eyes..........
Was already screaming his name right from the very beginning...........
If only , he would have cared or dared ....
To stare, glare or to have a glance or look ....
But how could he ever happen to read them..............
When he was already stuck and hooked.....
On some other beautiful book...ArVi…!!"

Arveena.

46

Merging Two Diverged Rivers Into An Ocean......

"And she said to him ....
But for how long you will stay away from me......??
When you know it quite well.......
That we both understand the depth of each other seas....
Let your wild emotions get merged in my deep emotions ......
By turning these two diverged rivers of love into one single divine ocean......
And prove to the world......
That sky and the sea do meet at some point is not a myth.................
But a nirvana, a pure devotion.... ArVi...!!"

Arveena.

47

Her Love And Her Light.......

"So when the sun will stop shining, i will become her moon.........

And when the moon will hide itself behind those dark clouds, i will strive to be her sun..........

Any time, any where ....every time ,every where.. In her deep love, i am always ready to burn............

Because i just can't bear to see her lost somewhere in the dark.........

Because i just can't bear to see her seeking for some another mesmerizing spark........

So as her best friend till the end i will fight.......

Just to make it sure that i am her only love, her only light...ArVi...!!"

Arveena.

48
Irony Of Love...........

"They just can't ache for you......
And they just can't feel your soul......
And you still expect them only to heal your soul............
They just can't love your imperfections.....
They just can't embrace your dark.......
And you still expect them only to be your only spark...
They just can't hear your silence.......
They just can't understand your heart.......
And you still expect them only to save you from falling apart...........
They just can't dance with you in rain.....
They just can't hold on to you in storm....
And see, you still want them only to be your only shelter...
Your only cozy home.....ArVi...!!"

Arveena.

49
Where Does All That Love Go......

"They asked her..............

But where does all that love go when it is not appreciated or reciprocated...........

Yeah, we really want to know where does all that lost love actually go..................

She thought for a while and then replied with a broken smile........

Some turn it into self love..........

Some feel it as their heartache forever ....

Some live it as their ultimate strength..........

Some turn it into never ending hate................

Some accept that loss as a part of their fate.....

Some hold onto it like some last undying hope............

Some let it kill them ....as if, it's their only addiction, drugs or dope.......

And then there are some deep, passionate and intense insane lovers come warriors like you and me.........

Who turn it into everything they can think, feel or imagine by turning it into their poetry............

So in real sense you never really lose love.............

How can you ever lose something that is itself a blessing from the heaven above.... ArVi..!!"

Arveena.

50

Love Lasts Even When Life Doesn't............

"To see her in pain and dancing all alone in the rain.....
He asked her..........
But why don't you forget about me......?
She sighed and replied........
Indeed, I will for sure...........
The day this mind will stop working........
And this heart will stop beating........
For you are the only secret of my soul..
That i will take with me to my grave.....ArVi...!! "

Arveena.

51
Leave Me Like........

"And she said to him.....
Leave me like the trees shed off and leave their trees....
In an autumn season with an intended purpose or reason..........
Slowly and steadily and with a gentle touch......
With no regrets and without hurting too much ....
With some grace and a fake smile on your face.......
Knowing deeply in your heart..........
That sometimes letting go......
Is the only wise decision.....ArVi....!! "

Arveena.

52
Love So Deep.....

"Love so deep.......

That every damn love they ever had before you…..

And every damn love they will ever have after you ………….

Turn shallow in front of you ………

Or otherwise don't love at all………………….

For if your love is not deep enough to leave it's mesmerizing mark……….

Just know that……..

It has already lost it's real worth………

Beauty, charm and spark….ArVi….!!"

Arveena.

53
Love Of A Poetess........

"And she said to him...........
Don't you ever underestimate , judge or test.......
Love of a poet or a poetess...........
For this deep blue ink of my pen.......
Will not get so easily drained ....
Unless or until ....
It leaves your heart marked and stained..............
Forever with my love.....ArVi...!!"

Arveena.

54
Mosaic........

"No breakage, just no real wreckage.........
Oh so guarded that you don't even dare to shatter or break..........
So tell me darling........
How can you expect yourself to turn out or become.......
Some beautiful mosaic......ArVi…!!"

Arveena.

55
Intrigued By Those Twinkling Stars......

"There is something too intriguing about those twinkling stars........
For the way they burn and shine.....
They inspire me and always make me believe..........
That fire in my soul.........
Can outshine every darkness that surrounds my misty grey sky..........
If only, i trust my own little spark....
And dare to burn for..........
What i love or believe in.....ArVi...!!"

Arveena.

56
Mind Vs Heart......

"Daily this mind and heart of mine ....
Goes for a non stop war.........
And daily both of them finally end up.........
Making peace with each other on these blank sheets of paper.........
Oh, only my god knows........
Who is going to win out of both........
Who is going to give up the fight.......
Who is wrong and who is really right........
I just can't explain how do i handle this struggle or battle....
For no one can really understand my plight....ArVi...!!"

Arveena.

57
Monday Morning...

"In a world seeking for dark and shady saturday nights with loud music and temporary hangovers...
She was someone like a serene and silent monday morning.....
Just too full of light....energy....beginnings...ambitions....and hopes .....
To be appreciated by all.....ArVi...!!"

Arveena.

58
Written In Braille.....

"And she said.........
So i am an open book........
Behind closed doors.......
Written in braille just for you.........
Read me as deeply as you can.......
As longer as you can............
Before the dawn breaks ....
And we both........
Finally wake up from our dreams of love..ArVi...!!"

Arveena.

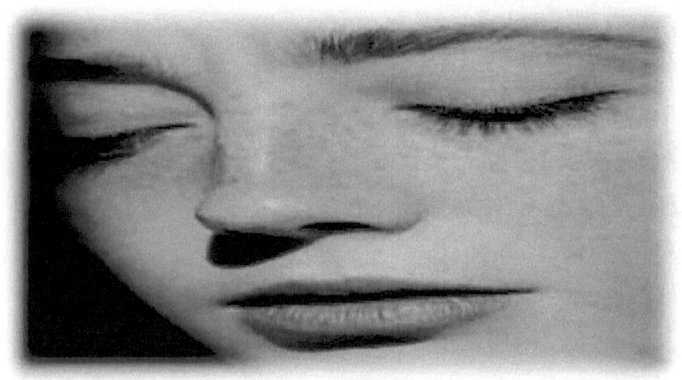

59

Forgetting Thee Feels Like....

"Forgetting thee feels like some old bonds or knots that has lost or loosened it's strong grip, but i am still unable to untie...

Like i am holding on to my merciless tears when all i want to do is to weep or cry....

Like the ocean of my raging emotions that always keeps on flowing nonstop is just about to run dry ...

Like someone clipped my beautiful invisible and invincible wings when i wanted to fly to touch the vast sky..........

And finally.............

Like the most beautiful ,mesmerizing and intoxicating hello i ever had...........

Is now finally telling me....it's time to say goodbye... .

Yeah, forgetting thee feels like some old bonds or knots that has lost or loosened it's strong grip, but i am still unable to untie..ArVi...!!"

Arveena.

60
Friendship Vs Love.....

"He always kept on telling me that i don't seem to understand that we are just friends ..

If only, he would have turned around ....

And instead of expecting me to understand would rather have tried once to understand me and my heart...

That for me, he has always been my love, my muse, my poetry and my art right from the very start.....

And see, it became more obvious for the way he left and slipped away like a splash of water or some grain of sand.....

That he has always been more like love and less like a friend...

For unlike love, friends never really leave your hand till the end....ArVi…!!"

Arveena.

61
She Finally Let Him Go........

"With forgiveness, gratitude And grace ....
And a little sad smile on her calm and serene face..........
She finally let him go.............
For she knew it damn well............
That her intense love was a madness........
That he could neither sustain nor he could ever contain.........
While she needed a daring as well as a caring heart.............
Who would not only appreciate her unconditional divine love ....
But will rather celebrate it like some blessing from the heaven above.....ArVi...!!"

Arveena.

62

His Undeniable Presence Or His Unbearable Absence....

"Lately..........
She spent her days and nights ....
Missing him and just writing about him...........
Unsure about her own vulnerable loving heart.............
Unware whether it was healing actually ......
Or was just falling apart.................
Unsure about his poetic personified existence........
Unaware what was bothering her the most......
His undeniable presence ....
Or his unbearable absence...ArVi..!!"

Arveena.

63
Her Silent Love Speaks To His Heart......

"But her silent love speaks to his heart.......
So loud and clear................
That it is just impossible for him ....not to hear...................
It is just impossible for him....not to care...................
For it is just inevitable for him....to be there.....................
For you just can't deny ....
The chemistry and the telepathy.. ....
When it is so deep, real, unique and rare....ArVi...!!"

Arveena.

64
He Left Me With So Much Of Poetry
(Diminishing Poem)

"He left me with so much of poetry that i can't delete it from my mind and heart and so i keep on mesmerizing it.....

He left me with so much of poetry that i can't delete it from my mind and heart.....

He left me with so much of poetry that i can't delete it......

He left me with so much of poetry.......

He left me with so much.........

He left me...........

He left.......ArVi....!!"

Arveena.

65
Being a Priority....

"They asked me..........
But what's so different and unique about your soulmate..............
I smiled and replied.........
Unlike all those guys who keep on telling me......
That I am different from the rest........
My beloved always says...........
That he never really noticed the rest.........
As for him.....I am the best...........ArVi...!!"

Arveena.

66
Ends Up To Your Pages....

"And I keep on telling my heart again and again...........
Whenever it's in too much distress or pain.......
Not to write about you anymore........
Not to love you that way to the core.......
But what to do......
My pen is much more stubborn than my heart ......
It finally ends up to your pages....... ArVi...!!"

Arveena.

67
Never Really Missing From Me......

"And after few years.......
When they finally met.........
He asked her.........
But how would i believe that you truly loved me......
When even after so much of time and distance between us ....
You have never really missed me at all........
Wondering at his question as well as expression.......
She hugged him tight and replied.......
Coz even after so much of time and distance between us ......
You were never really missing from me at all....ArVi…!!"

Arveena.

68
The Glue......

"She sighed and whispered..........
But i just can't let you in............
For my heart is already in thousands bits and scattered pieces........
And there is just no place or space left for someone new.........
Trust me it's true................
He smiled and replied..............
Then let me be the glue ..ArVi...!!"

Arveena.

69
Turn Them Into Your Poetry...

"Some people feel like.....

Everything you have ever found and everything you have ever lost in love.....

Together one at the same time.......

And might be that's why.........

Yeah, might be that's why........

Before they fade away like some blurred memory......

You make them eternal by turning them into your poetry.......ArVi...!!"

Arveena.

70
Everything Tragically And Terrifically Beautiful About Her....

"There was nothing really gorgeous.......
But everything tragically and terrifically beautiful about her.........
Beauty that sounds constructive at times......
Beauty that sounds destructive at times........
Like darkness....
Like silence .....
Like some forest fire.................
Like some wild adventure...........
Like those wild flowers..........
Like danger.....
Like dreams................
Like an unrequited love ....
Like passions ....
Like pains.................
Like poetry...................
Yeah...........
There was nothing really gorgeous.......
But everything tragically and terrifically beautiful about her.......ArVi...!!"

Arveena.

71
Love Is Never About....

"Love is never about holding each other's hands, but about holding each other's heart....

Never about taking each other's breath away, but about becoming each other's reason to breathe.......

Never about turning each other insane, but about becoming each other's sanity in darkness and pain.........

And above all, it's never about ignoring each other just to catch each other's attention......

But about giving so much attention that they just can't ignore you even if they wish to......

And yes, one has to learn first what love is not about.......

Before you finally understand what love is all about......ArVi...!!"

Arveena.

72
She Keeps On Filling.....

"And no matter how many characters choose to walk away from her very chapters.......
None of her canvas will be ever blank....
And none of her life book pages will be ever empty...
For she keeps on filling them time and again........
With her art, her passions and her poetry....ArVi...!!"

Arveena.

73
In Each Other's Thoughts And Prayers....

"She was too wild and free to be caged, possessed or tamed........
And he was too wise and tamed to run wild with her..............
So anyway, they couldn't keep each other...........
Oh, but the way they kept each other in their thoughts and prayers.......
It was profound and magnificent......ArVi...!!"

Arveena.

74
How Stubborn Your Love Is.......

"How stubborn your love is , like the waves in the sea.....
It comes and goes......
Everytime leaving me just standstill.....
Tides of emotions fly so high.....
Only to fall again once more.....
Into heartaches of indifference and silence between both of us ....
Sailing in two different worlds ....
And somehow, i hate to swim anymore.....
So let me get drown to the core.....
Before you leave me alone at the shore.....ArVi…!!"

Arveena.

75
Stuck On Love..........

"But his memories no more rain over me...
Infact, many of them faded away........
With those continuous strong and hard blow of winds.......
That i faced alone when his heart turned into stone.......
Still don't know why ....
My sky is always surrounded by ....
Dark and dense clouds of his love ...
As if , he is the only storm ....
My desert heart needs .....
To save it from getting abandoned......ArVi...!!"

Arveena.

76
But I Love Him.....

"And she said...........
But i love him.........
Just like the clouds love the rain.......
Just like a masochistic love the pain.....
Just like the oceans love the storm.....
And i am as much confident about the power of my own love......
As much i am secured to always let him go.............
For i know no matter what.....
No one can ever stay away for too long.....
From his or her cozy sweet home.....ArVi…!!"

Arveena.

77
Loving You Even More......

"Like those stubborn, vigorous, stormy.....
Turbulent, unruly ,unstoppable tidal waves................
I keep on crashing again and again.......
Back to your damn shore...............
Oh, everytime I try to hate you.....
Forget about you or get over you.............
I just end up loving you even more..ArVi...!!"

Arveena .

78
Find Someone Who Feels Like Some Love Song.....

"And she whispered........
So find someone who sounds and feels like some love song .....
And then keep on dancing to the rhythm of his or her love.........
Yeah, stay drunk on his or her music, lyrics, silence as well as melodious voice......
In a world full of people who are nothing more than some meaningless noise......ArVi…!!"

Arveena.

79
Waves Of An Ocean....

"Her mind and her heart always follow.......
The trends of the waves of an ocean.......
Never really too calm..........
Never really intended to harm...........
Oh, only those who dares to dive in ....
Really know about the hidden treasures...
That are found in their mysterious depths....ArVi..!!"

Arveena.

80

In Every Love Story....

"And the writer said..........

In every love story behind it's every dark mystery......

There is some terrific history.........

For some, love was just too shallow to hold on, so they gave up too soon..............

While for others , it was just too hard to let it go.......

Because of it's damn strong chemistry......ArVi...!!"

Arveena.

81
Hidden Treasures...

" I am neither diving nor drowning........
But still learning to swim in it's strong waves..........
For the ocean of love is too deep and vast to explore. .....
And i won't stop irrespective of all those strong waves, tides and storms.......
Until i reach the sea beds. .....
And get all it's hidden treasures.......ArVi...!!"

Arveena.

82
Promise...

"Never ever promise anyone......

That you will always be there for someone if you don't really mean it.....

Because they can do the craziest thing of their life......

Like taking it seriously and believing it true forever......

For promise might be a small word for you to make something.....

But it may turn out as the biggest word for them to break their almost everything....ArVi...!!"

Arveena.

83
Immortal Love...

"Let it go, let it die.....
Even let them try to bury it alive......
For what is love will always grow, stay and survive ....
Facing all the storms, earthquakes and tsunamis of life........
With all it's gratitude and grace...........
And if anyway it has already died ......
Just know that ......
It was never really love at the first place....ArVi...!!"

Arveena.

84
Love Poem She Is.....

"Music that needs no lyrics........
And lyrics that need no music.........
Too whole for she was too full of heart and soul.......
All blazing fire, passion and pain basking in unfathomable glory.........
Indeed, deep down inside, she knew it damn well................
That she herself is the kind of deep love poem......
That just won't fit in any ordinary life book of any ordinary life story.......ArVi...!!"

Arveena.

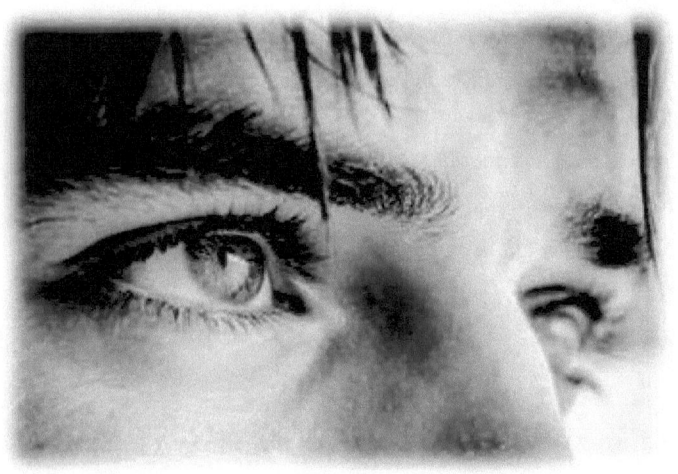

85
Thou Eyes...

"Thou eyes are like mysterious raging oceans of hidden emotions........
And those dark circles and wrinkles right below them.........
Are nothing but the ripple effects they make....
On the stormy waves of my restless heart........
And you still wonder..............
How loving thee is a poetry to me..............
How loving you unconditionally .....
Always feel like some real magic , some abstract art ...ArVi....!!"

Arveena.

86
Solace....

"And in your absence......
Considering and judging me as a free, lost and lonely bird ....
Flying and flying just aimlessly and hopelessly..........
Everyone around me decorated their trees and branches........
With beautiful fragrances and flowers to their best.......
With the hope.......
That i might get fascinated by their beauty and i might take some rest... ...
But how could i even think of stopping somewhere else.........
When it's in your heart only......
That i found my home, my real nest..ArVi…!!"

Arveena.

87

Her Love Is Divine....

"And he said....
Even my whole world turns upside down...
Baby, whenever you are with me, I feel just perfectly alright and fine........
It's the way you caress my heart and soul while embracing my darkness.......
Just your mere presence in my life puts me on cloud number mine......
As sweet as sugar, as addictive as my favourite vodka or wine....
Oh , everytime your crimson rosy petals touches mine and our breaths finally entwine........
It brings chills and shivers up and down to my spine.........
What else would i say, your aroma is so spiritual and magical ......
That i am always lost in mesmerizing thoughts of thine.........
Had i been a poet, i would have written an anthology on you.........
But you are yourself nothing less than some love poem for me .....
That i keep on mesmerizing day and night...
So anything i say in your honour my beloved, my demise....
It would be an understatement just would not suffice....
So just one word to define your deep unconditional love.....
Divine.........ArVi…!!"

Arveena.

88
Book Lover....

"At night, when I sleep....
I keep him close just next to my heart.....
And in the morning, i just keep on writing and reading him to save myself from falling apart........
Chapter by chapter , paragraph by paragraph, phrase by phrase and word by word......
That's how i fill in all the blank spaces in my life book.....
For i am madly and badly stuck on his pages......
As he is the only book i will never ever put down....
Oh, totally spellbound and lost ....
In his love and it's everlasting glory.......
So there is just no question of reading or writing......
Some another love story...ArVi...!!"

Arveena.

89
Wild And Dense Forest....

"My heart is now a unique, wild and dense forest......
Where wild flowers of your love bloom and blossom on their own.........
Irrespective of rains , storms, sunshine, seasons, reasons and so on....
Come and see.......
Initials of your love have got engraved and carved......
On almost each and every tree.....
So if you really want me to forget about you or get over you........
You have to cut all the branches and deep roots of your love.. ......
And dig down deeper......
To take out all seeds of your friendship...moments and memories shared......
To finally set my soul free......ArVi...!!"

Arveena.

90
Love Is A Raging Fire....

"Oh no darling.......
Love is neither a dream nor a desire.......
But a raging fire.........
Where weak hearts explode.........
Strong hearts melt........
And those strongest ones burn on and on and on.....
Until and unless they burn themselves down to their ashes......
To rise once again ....
Like the phoenix they already are.......ArVi…!!"

Arveena.

91
Love Her Loud....

"Read her eyes, know her heart.....

And most importantly, try to know her darkest and wildest side......

And that's how you will really know her....

And when you have finally got to know her....

Trap her mind, touch her soul, caress her heart...

Care for her and chase her, as if you are still trying to get her.....

And that's how for forever, you will really keep her ......

Just like an artist is obsessive about his or her heart.....

Just like a passionate lover is obsessive about his or her beloved's heart....ArVi...!!"

Arveena.

92
She Is Made Up Of....

"Indeed, she is made up of.........
All the places she ever visited......
All the people she ever loved........
All the songs she ever heard......
All the secrets she ever kept........
All the tears she ever wept..........
All the hearts she ever touched.........
All the moments she ever treasured.....
All the memories she ever made........
All the poems she ever wrote.........
And all the fights she ever fought....ArVi...!!"

Arveena.

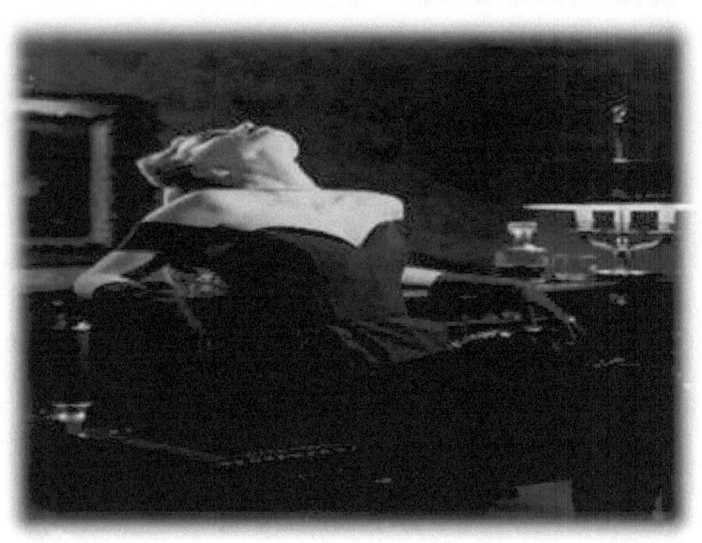

93

Being An Extremist And An Empath..

"Yes, she is an extremist and an empath too....
She loves too much, she feels too much...
She trusts too much, she cares too much..........
She thinks too much and bears too much.......
So no other flowers but only roses grow.....
In the garden of her heart........
Spreading eternal fragrance of love all around the world.....
Lifting and putting up together all those souls that have fallen apart....
Sounds so beautiful, but what about the thorns?
Oh, don't worry, she keeps them with herself......
So can you now feel her pains?
Can you see how she dances madly all alone in the heavy rains?
Still proud of each and every thorn ....
Wound, scar or pain.....
For they all made her what she is today.......
And none of her heartache or pain has ever gone in vain......ArVi...!!"

Arveena.

94
I Will Let You Set The Pace....

"Sometimes I love you....
Sometimes I am just so scared of you. ....
Every time you come closer, my heart beats go faster.....
Oh my darling, you are such a terrific and beautiful disaster....
Should l call you my lover, my monster or my beast.....
Whatever the hell you are, you cast such a magical spell upon me...
That I am always ready to become your prey , your feast......
I know your love will either save me or destroy me....
But i just can't run away from you, no matter how much you annoy me...
Every move your side turns me crazy, makes me insane,
I just can't standstill.....
As if, i am hypnotized by your destiny, and to get you,
I will cross all hurdles, will climb almost every mountain or hill.....
In my whole life, i have never met someone ....
Who is so attractive, mysterious, strong , playful, addictive and wild....
You arouse a woman's passion for love in a girl......
Who, before meeting you was so sane and innocent like a child....
So now unless and until i get you.....
Twenty four by seven, you are on my head....

I am just amazed at your glory, your unique charm, your hypnotizing eyes and your overall grace.......

So baby , bring it on…!!

Trust me, this time, i will let you set the pace..ArVi…!!"

Arveena.

95
Loving You In My Dreams.

"And so, I choose to love you only in my fantasies, desires and dreams...

For your reality just doesn't fit in mine.......

They say, dreams have no expiry date.........

So might be that's way, loving you forever is now written in my fate......

Unless and until you yourself come over one day, break this killing silence.......

Finally wake me up and shatter all my hopelessly romantic dreams about thee....

And turn this forever kind of love into a never ending kind of hate.......

Till then, i choose to firmly hold on to you my beloved ......

Yes till then, i choose to dream about you and just wait.....ArVi...!!"

Arveena.

96
Where Can We Find True Love?

"They asked me, so where can we find true love.....
I smiled and replied, in every single blessing you ever had from the heaven above....
You will find it in a child's smile and the way he or she learns to overcome his fears.....
You will find it in a mother's warm embrace when she hugs her child to wipe off his or her tears......
You will find it in the sound of crashing waves when they hit the shore of a raging ocean....
You will find it in a lover's eyes in it's every silent and hidden emotion....
It's always there somewhere in that pouring rain....
It's always there somewhere in someone 's sadness or pain....
It's in those strong bonds of friendship that we share....
And the way we selflessly love, give and care....
It's still beating there in hearts that are not broken yet but just bent..
It's still beating there in every goodbye said thousands of times but never really meant...
It's hidden somewhere even in your anger and that hate....
You just can't separate yourself from this feeling, for it's written very much in your destiny and fate.....
Trust me, it's so powerful that even in darkness or silence, it can be apparently seen and loudly heard.....
So tell me, can't you feel it right now, breathing endlessly damn alive in my every single written word...ArVi....!!"

Arveena.

97
Museum.

"She pushes them all away, still none of them dares to walk away........

She warns them all to stay away..............

Still all they want is to sway and stay...............

Oh so obvious for them, not to get away.......

For it's hard to leave and walk away from the only damn unique place........

That feels like some museum.......

In a world so full of empty hallways...ArVi…!!"

Arveena.

98
Crescent Full Moon....

"But thee rose like a crescent full moon in my dark blue and grey vast sky........

As if someone has greeted me with a sweet hello after thousands of harsh goodbyes...

Like finding an immense happiness after long intervals of heartaches and pains........

Like an unexpected rainbow appears out of nowhere, after long intervals of sun shines and rains.....

Thee look like a blessing, i am not yet ready to receive.........

Thee feel like a promise , i am not yet ready to believe....ArVi...!!"

Arveena.

99
Love....

"I can make you stumble ....

I can make you fall....

I can make you feel empty or whole at times...

For without me, your life is nothing at all..

I am your happiness...

I am your pain...

I am your sunshine...

I am your rain....

I am the storm...

I am the cloud...

I am the silent voice of your heart..

That's keep on hitting you like your favourite music playing around just too loud....

I am your whole journey...

I am your final destination...

I am infinite, eternal...

My depth is just beyond your imagination...

I am your beginning ,i am your start....

I am your end, i am your final stop....

I am both your terrific nightmare as well as your lovely dream...

Give up on everything you wish to, but don't you dare to give up on me, for i am your only hope...

I am the path you all want to traverse....
I am the moment once gone....
You can only mesmerize and miss but can't repeat or reverse... ...
I am the music that keeps on playing in your head...
When I touch your life, you feel alive...
But when i leave, you feel almost half dead...
At times, i turn out your greatest blessing.....
But to feel me too deeply can turn out as curse....
Yes, I am love....
The whole world knows me...
Still don't know that i am the soul of the entire universe...ArVi...!!"

Arveena.

100
Bookmark....

"You are like a bookmark in the storybook of my life.......
Holding little space, still too significant to lose..........
A constant reminder of ....
where i was, where i am and where i am going ahead in my life..........
As if, without you and your existence..............
I will get lost somewhere....
in my own damn pages.......ArVi...!!"

Arveena.

www.ingramcontent.com/pod-product-compliance
Lightning Source LLC
LaVergne TN
LVHW041705070526
838199LV00045B/1213